My Family Helps Me

Healthy Living

Here is my family.

My mom is in my family.

My dad is in my family.

My sister is
in my family, too.

Dad helps me
to do a puzzle.

11

Mom helps me
to make the pancakes.

My sister helps me
to use the computer.

My family helps me to do lots of things.